Nocturnal Animals

by Ann M. Rossi

What You Already Know

There are many different kinds of animals. The different kinds of animals can be put into groups.

One group of animals has backbones. Mammals have backbones. So do most birds, fish, reptiles, and amphibians.

Another group of animals does not have backbones. Insects do not have backbones.

Animals in all groups are adapted to different kinds of environments.

beetle

Some animals change color to hide from predators. This is one kind of camouflage. Fish are adapted to live in water. Fish have gills to help them get oxygen from the water. Each kind of animal is adapted to live in its environment.

The animals in this book are also adapted to live in their environment. They are adapted to be active at night.

moth

Nocturnal Animals

Have you ever been outside at night and heard animal noises? Maybe you have seen an animal moving around in the dark. Maybe you have heard animal noises near you. Not all animals sleep at night. Some animals rest in the daytime and use the night for finding food and hunting prey.

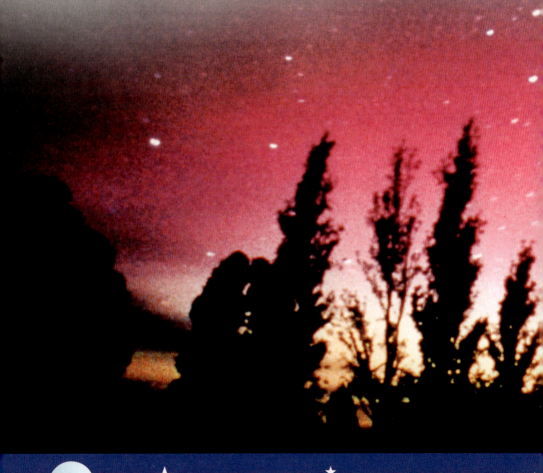

Animals that find food and move around at night are called nocturnal animals. Nocturnal animals can be found in many different habitats. Animals such as desert hamsters, scorpions, owls, fireflies, coyotes, bats, and red-eyed tree frogs are nocturnal.

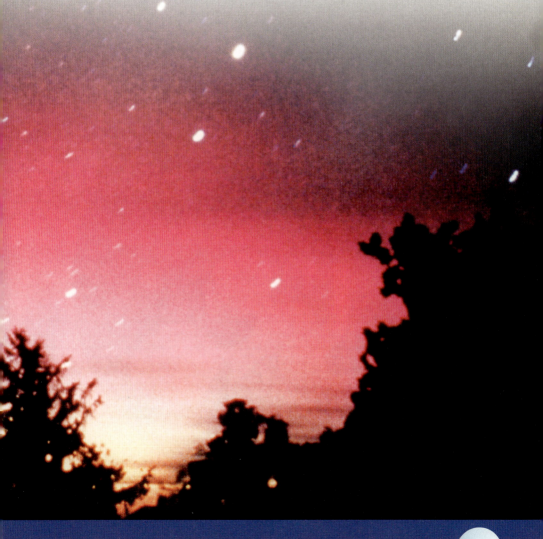

Desert Hamsters

Desert hamsters are small mammals that live in the desert. They are well adapted to life in this environment. Desert hamsters want to keep out of the heat and light of the desert in the daytime. They dig underground burrows. Each desert hamster spends the daytime hours sleeping in its own deep burrow.

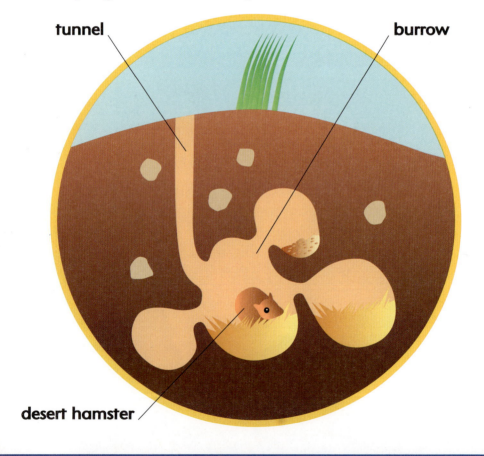

Desert hamsters come out of their burrows at night to find food. Their back feet are furry to protect them from hot desert sand. Desert hamsters eat seeds. They also eat fruit, leaves, stems, and buds. Sometimes, desert hamsters eat insects.

Scorpions

Scorpions also live in the desert. Scorpions might look like insects, but they are arachnids. Arachnids have four sets of legs and two body parts. Spiders, mites, and ticks are also arachnids.

Like desert hamsters, scorpions spend the daytime out of the hot desert sun. During the day, scorpions find cool, shady places to sleep. They sleep in cracks of wood. They sleep inside and under rocks.

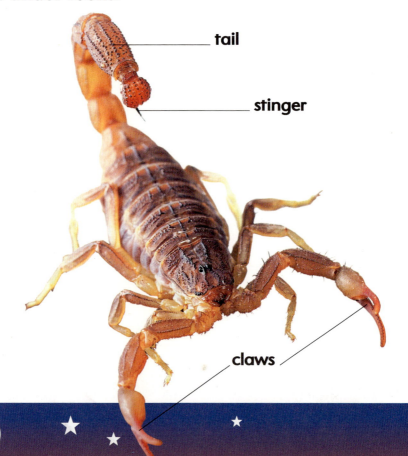

At night, scorpions come out to look for food. They eat insects, spiders, centipedes, earthworms, and other scorpions. They use their claws to catch their prey. Scorpions inject poison into their prey with the stinger in their tail.

Owls

Most owls are nocturnal animals. Owls live in many different habitats. During the day, they sleep in hollow trees or holes in rocky cliffs.

When night comes, owls are ready to go hunting. They see well in the dark. They also hear very well. Some owls can find mice just by hearing them run.

These birds are carnivores, or meat eaters. Most owls catch live animals to eat, like mice, gophers, and small birds. They swoop down silently. They use their claws, called talons, to grab their prey. Some kinds of owls look for prey while flying high in the air. Other owls look for prey on the ground.

Fireflies

Fireflies also fly around at night looking for food. These nocturnal insects live in many habitats, but most fireflies are found in warm damp places.

Fireflies mostly live near streams and ponds. They spend their days sleeping in bushes near the water. The fireflies on the right live in a cave.

At night, young fireflies look for earthworms, snails, and slugs to eat. Older fireflies eat plant nectar.

Have you ever seen a firefly at night? Flickering lights can be seen as they zip through the night sky. They have body parts that can give off a light signal. This light helps them warn away predators. It also helps them communicate with other fireflies.

Coyotes

Do you know what these animals are? They are coyotes! Like owls and fireflies, coyotes live in many different habitats. These nocturnal mammals spend most days sleeping in dens. Coyotes usually dig their own dens. Sometimes, they will take holes made by other animals and make them bigger. Sometimes, coyotes will make dens in holes in rocky ledges.

Coyotes spend most nights hunting in groups of twos and threes. Coyotes will eat almost anything they are able to chew. They eat rabbits, squirrels, other small mammals, insects, reptiles, and fruit.

Coyotes hear well. They listen to find prey and to keep away from danger.

Bats

What is that animal hanging upside-down? It is a bat! These flying mammals are also nocturnal. They live in many different habitats too.

Most bats hang upside-down to rest in the daytime. They may sleep in trees, caves, or attics. Some kinds of bats sleep hanging by one foot!

Bats eat all kinds of food. Some bats eat insects, scorpions, or spiders. Others eat fruit. There are even bats that catch fish, lizards, small birds, or tree frogs. Bats can find food on the ground, on plants, and in the air.

Many bats use their sense of smell to find food. Others use echolocation. This means that when these bats fly they make sounds that echo, or bounce off, objects. The bat can tell where the objects are. This way, they can find their prey in the dark.

Red-eyed Tree Frogs

The red-eyed tree frog is another nocturnal animal. Like some bats, the red-eyed tree frog lives in a tropical environment. This kind of amphibian lives in rain forests in Central and South America.

Red-eyed tree frogs hunt for prey at night. Like some of the other animals you have read about, red-eyed tree frogs are carnivores. They eat crickets, moths, flies, grasshoppers, and even other frogs.

Red-eyed tree frogs live in trees. When they sleep during the day, their green coloring helps to camouflage them in the leaves. This way, they can try to stay safe from predators that hunt in the daytime.

Sometimes, predators are not fooled by the red-eyed tree frog's camouflage. If a predator gets too close, the frog wakes up. When the frog's eyes pop open, their shining red color scares away the predator.

cricket

There are nocturnal creatures in almost every group of animals. There are many nocturnal animals that have backbones. The panther is a nocturnal mammal. The kiwi is a nocturnal bird. The angel shark is a nocturnal fish. The crocodile is a nocturnal reptile. The toad is a nocturnal amphibian.

panther

There are also many nocturnal animals that do not have backbones. The moth is a nocturnal insect. The earthworm is a nocturnal worm.

moth

crocodile

Nocturnal animals are found in many different environments. Nocturnal animals live on the ground, in the air, and in the ocean. Some of these creatures are adapted for life where it is hot. Others are adapted for life where it is cold. Nocturnal animals can live where it is wet and where it is dry.

Each kind of animal has special adaptations that help it live in its environment. But nocturnal creatures are alike in one very important way. They are all adapted for life at night.

Glossary

arachnids   animals with four pairs of legs and two main body parts

burrows   holes or tunnels dug by small animals and used as homes or shelters

carnivores   meat-eating animals

echolocation   the way animals such as bats and dolphins use their senses to find other objects in their environment

nocturnal   most active at night

talons   the claws of predatory birds like owls and eagles